I am lāt_e. I āt_e ham

I āt_e and āt_e. and now I am

lāt_e. I will run.

I wish I had sand. I wish I had a rāk_e. I wish I had a fish. I wish I had a lāk_e.

hē has a fat cat. hē has fun with his fat cat.

his mom has a littlₑ cat. shē has fun with thē littlₑ cat. thē littlₑ cat has fun in thē sand.

a littlₑ fish sat on a fat fish.

thē littlₑ fish said, "wow."

thē littlₑ fish did not hāte thē

fat fish. thē littlₑ fish said,

"that fat fish is mom."

thē cow sat on a gāte. thē cow said, "thē gāte is hot." shē said, "I hāte hot gātes."

a fish āt_e a roc_k. thē fish

said, "I āt_e a roc_k."

a cow āt_e thē fish. thē cow

said, "I āt_e a fish. and now I

fēēl sic_k."

shē can kick. shē can lick. shē

said, "I am not a cat." shē said,

"I am not a fish."

is shē a man?

shē was not mad at him. did

shē hit him? nō, nō, nō. did shē

hug him? nō, nō, nō. did shē

kiss him?

hē said, "can I ēₐt a nut?"

shē said, "gō sit with thē

cow."

hē said, "nō. I will not gō."

shē said, "gō sit with thē cat."

hē said, "thē cat can ēₐt a nut."

shē said, "gō sit with thē cat

and ē‌ₐt."

sō hē āt‌ₑ a nut. hē said, "this is

fun."

hē has nō fēēt. hē has nō

nōse. hē has nō tēēth. hē is not

a cow. and hē is not a cat.

is hē a rat? nō. hē is not a

rat.

I can kiss a cat. I can kiss

a kitt_en.

can a cow kiss mē? nō. a cow

can not kiss mē. a cow can

lic_k mē.

can a cat lic_k a kitt_en?

I hav_e a cow. thē cow is fat.

I hav_e a cat. thē cat is fat.

how can I tāk_e thē cow and

thē cat with mē? can thē cow

sit on thē cat? nō.

wē havₑ hats. I can hōld thē

hats. thē cow can hōld thē hats.

an ōld man can hōld thē hats.

can a fat rat hōld thē hats?

wē sāv_e roc_ks. wē sāv_e sac_ks

and sac_ks of roc_ks. wē sāv_e

lots and lots of roc_ks.

wē hav_e lots of littl_e roc_ks.

wē sit on roc_ks. and wē giv_e

an ōld man lots of roc_ks.

the ōld man said, "I can

shāve a cat." sō hē did.

the ōld man said, "I can shāve

a cow." sō hē did.

the ōld man said, "I can shāve

a rock."

did hē shāv_e a roc_k? nō.

hē said, "givₑ mē a hat ōr a

sock." sō shē gāvₑ him a sock

fōr his nōsₑ.

hē said, "I nēₑd socks on thē

fēēt, not on thē nōsₑ." sō shē

gāvₑ him socks fōr his fēēt.

thē ōld man was cōld. hē did

not havₑ a hat ōr a cō₍ₐ₎t ōr socₖs.

sō hē got a gō₍ₐ₎t with lots of

hats and cō₍ₐ₎ts and socₖs.

now thē ōld man is not cōld

and thē gō₍ₐ₎t is not cōld.

the ōld gō_at had an ōld cō_at.

the ōld gō_at said, "I will ē_at this

ōld cō_at." sō shē did.

"that was fun," shē said. "I āt_e

the ōld cō_at. and now I am cōld."

now the ōld gō_at is sad.

the fat man and his fat cow

got on a little rock.

a cat said, "fat man, that rock

will not hold a fat man and his

cow. that rock will go down

the hill."

did thē rocₖ gō down thē hill

with thē fat man and his fat

cow?

thē rat had fun. hē ran in thē sand.

hē had sand on his fēēt. hē had sand on his ēars. hē had sand on his nōse. hē had sand on his tāil.

hē said, "I havₑ a lot of sand ⟶

on mē." ⟶

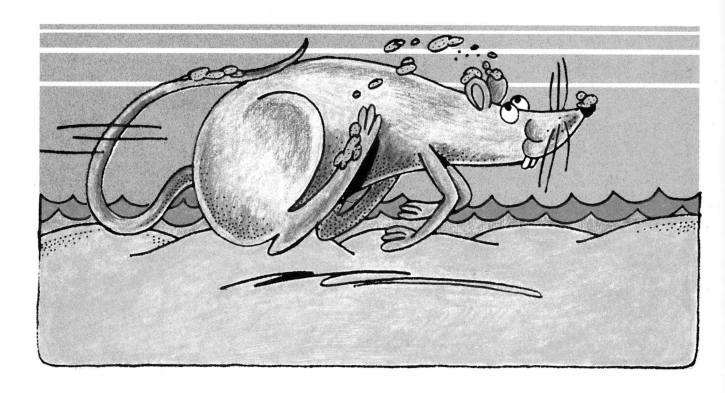

shē said, "I havₑ a fan."

hē said, "I havₑ sand."

shē said, "wē can run thē

sand in thē fan." sō hē ran thē

fan nēₐr thē sand.

hē had sand in his ēₐrs. hē

said, "I can not hēₐr." →

hē had sand on his sēₐt. shē →

said, "wē havₑ sand on us." →

a dog sat in a littlₑ car. thē

dog said, "I nēēd to ēₐt."

will thē dog ēₐt a fish? nō.

will thē dog ēₐt a log? nō. will

thē dog ēₐt a pot of tar? nō.

thē dog will ēₐt thē car.

a dog was in thē fog. a cat
was in thē fog. a gōat was in
thē fog.

thē dog and thē cat and thē
gōat cāme to a log.

thē cat and thē dog sat on thē

log. thē dog and thē cat said,

"wē arₑ on thē log."

thē gōat said, "I am not on

thē log. I am in thē log. ha ha."

the fat man and his dog had

a car. the car did not run.

so the fat man and his dog

got a goat. the fat man and

his dog sat on the goat. the goat

did not go.

the͞e fat man said, "the͞e go͞at
will not go͞."

so͞ the͞e fat man and his dog
sat on the͞e ro͞ad.

lots of cars

a man on a farm has lots of

cars. hē has ōld cars. hē has

littl e cars.

ar e his cars fōr gōa ts? nō.

are his cars fōr shēēp? nō. are

his cars fōr cows? nō.

his cars are fōr cops. hē has

lots of cop cars.

thē girl and thē dog

thē girl said, "I can tēₐch thē

dog to run."

thē dog said, "nō."

thē girl said, "I will tēₐch thē

dog to run."

thē dog said, "nō. thē girl can
not tēₐch mē to run. I can run.
ha ha."

a girl in a cāve

a girl was in a cāve. a wāve cāme in the cāve. the girl said, "sāve mē, sāve mē."

a fish cāme in the cāve. she

said, "I will sāve that girl."

and shē did.

  thē fish said, "now I will give

that girl a sēēd and a ham to

ēat." sō shē gāve thē girl a sēēd

and a ham.